The
Sound of Leadership

The Sound of Leadership

Edvante M. Showers

Published by Game Changer Publishing

Paperback ISBN: 978-1-962656-81-8
Hardcover ISBN: 978-1-962656-82-5
Digital: ISBN: 978-1-962656-83-2

www.GameChangerPublishing.com

DEDICATION

To Sage, may the words of my present create a LEGACY that cultivates your future. When you feel like you hit the glass ceiling, my hope is that you build a bigger building. Dream BIG; anything is POSSIBLE!

The
Sound of Leadership

Edvante M. Showers

www.GameChangerPublishing.com

Table of Contents

Introduction

In the vast landscape of organizations, leadership is the unseen force that unites different aspects, forming a unified and sturdy structure. It serves as the directing power that advances a shared vision, overcoming obstacles and guiding toward achievement. Leadership is more than just a role; it's an *active* impact that establishes the mood for the entire organization.

At its essence, effective leadership is akin to a skilled conductor orchestrating a symphony. It harmonizes the diverse talents and perspectives within a team, creating a melody that transcends individual contributions. A leader's influence resonates in strategic decisions and how they inspire and motivate each team member to perform at their best.

Leadership is the beacon that illuminates the path forward, providing clarity and direction. It instills a sense of purpose, transforming tasks into meaningful contributions towards a shared goal. A great leader not only articulates this vision but also embodies it, becoming a source of inspiration for others to follow.

In times of uncertainty, leadership is the steady hand that steers the ship. It embraces change with adaptability, turning challenges into opportunities for growth. A resilient leader fosters an environment where the team feels supported, encouraging them to confront adversity with courage and determination.

The value of leadership extends beyond the balance sheets and spreadsheets. It encompasses the human element, recognizing the strengths and potential of each team member. A leader's ability to cultivate a positive and inclusive culture fosters a sense of belonging, elevating the team from basic coordination to harmonious collaboration.

Ultimately, leadership is a continuous composition, a journey rather than a destination. It is about learning, evolving, and inspiring others to do the same. In the ever-changing dynamics of the organizational landscape, effective leadership is the constant that propels teams toward innovation, resilience, and enduring success.

Let's step into the world of leadership—a dynamic force that shapes the very fabric of organizations. Imagine it as an invisible thread weaving through the diverse elements, creating a resilient tapestry. In this book, we will delve into the profound value of leadership—a force that transcends roles and positions, steering teams toward success and fostering a culture of collaboration. Picture leadership not just as a position but as a symphony conductor, orchestrating a harmonious melody from the diverse talents within a team. It illuminates the path forward, providing clarity, purpose, and inspiration.

Join this journey as we examine the challenges of leadership and how overcoming them becomes a catalyst for growth, resilience, and enduring success.

CHAPTER 1

Defining Leadership

Leadership is more than just a title. At its core, leadership is the art of casting a vision that guides and inspires. Through exploring stories of visionaries, this chapter highlights the profound impact leaders can have when *affluence* and *influence* harmonize. Remember, in the leadership realm, it's not about the title you hold; it's about the vision you unfold.

This leads us to the crucial intersection of affluence and influence. Successful leaders are not only distinguished by their ability to articulate a compelling vision but also by their capacity to wield affluence and influence in tandem. Affluence, beyond monetary wealth, encompasses a wealth of resources—intellectual, emotional, and relational—that leaders leverage to bring their vision to life.

Here are a few examples of successful leaders who have mastered the relationship between affluence and influence:

"Someone's sitting in the shade today because someone planted a tree a long time ago." - Warren Buffett

Warren Buffett himself exemplifies this quote through his actions. Known not only for his immense wealth but also for his philanthropic efforts, Buffett pledged to give away over 99% of his fortune to philanthropic causes, primarily via the Gates Foundation, influencing positive change and investing in the future.

"As we look ahead into the next century, leaders will be those who empower others." - Bill Gates

Bill Gates, through the Bill & Melinda Gates Foundation, has used his wealth to tackle global health issues, education, and poverty, empowering organizations and individuals through grants and programs, thereby showcasing how influence and affluence can be utilized to empower and uplift others.

"Leadership is about empathy. It is about having the ability to relate to and connect with people for the purpose of inspiring and empowering their lives." - Oprah Winfrey

Oprah Winfrey, a media mogul and philanthropist, uses her platform and resources to inspire and empower others. Her charitable work, including her leadership academy for girls in South Africa, demonstrates how affluence and influence can be used to make a significant impact on the lives of others.

"The ability to deal with people is as purchasable a commodity as sugar or coffee, and I will pay more for that ability than for any other under the sun." - John D. Rockefeller

Rockefeller, one of the richest individuals in history, was known not only for his immense wealth but also for his philanthropy. His establishment of foundations that focused on public health, education, and scientific research showed his understanding of the importance of using influence and resources for the greater good.

"Do what you can, with what you have, where you are."
- Theodore Roosevelt

Theodore Roosevelt used his position of influence, both as a president and a public figure, to advocate for progressive policies and conservation efforts. His leadership style and dedication to using his influence for public service serve as a prime example of how leaders can use their position and resources to effect change.

Let's turn our attention to the heart of leadership—the ability to cast a compelling vision. A clear vision serves as the North Star, providing direction and purpose. It's about articulating goals and painting a vivid picture that ignites passion and commitment. A powerful vision serves as a magnetic force that unites teams and propels individuals toward common goals.

In the upcoming sections, we'll journey through the intricacies of crafting and communicating a vision that resonates. Remember, in the symphony of leadership, vision isn't just a note; it's the melody that echoes across boundaries, inspiring harmony and orchestrating success.

Leadership vision is about specificity—how a crystal-clear vision acts as a beacon that guides decisions and actions. Clarity is not just a concept but a catalyst for change.

It's essential to dissect what sets extraordinary leadership apart. Extraordinary leaders not only cast a vision; they breathe life into it, infusing it with passion and authenticity. They go beyond the ordinary, transforming challenges into opportunities and inspiring others to do the same. It's not just about achieving goals but leaving an enduring legacy.

There are several key characteristics that distinguish a leader who transcends the ordinary:

- *Passionate Conviction:*

  Extraordinary leaders exude a passionate commitment to their vision, igniting a fire within themselves and those around them.

- *Authenticity:*

  They lead with authenticity, aligning their actions with their values and creating a genuine connection with their teams.

- *Innovative Resilience:*

  Extraordinary leaders navigate challenges with innovative resilience, turning setbacks into stepping stones toward their vision.

- *Inclusive Collaboration:*

  They foster an inclusive environment, recognizing that diverse perspectives fuel creativity and propel their vision forward.

- *Enduring Legacy:*

  Extraordinary leaders envision beyond immediate success, crafting a legacy that extends beyond their time, inspiring generations to come.

- *Adaptive Vision:*

  They possess an adaptive vision, recognizing the evolving landscape and adjusting their course without compromising their core principles.

- *Empowering Others:*

  Extraordinary leaders empower others to contribute to the vision, creating a collective force that amplifies the impact.

We want to understand what makes great leadership by examining its key features. This will give us a deeper understanding of what truly makes a leader effective and inspiring.

Extraordinary leaders make their vision clear through a combination of strategic communication, vivid storytelling, and unwavering commitment. They employ several tactics to ensure their vision is not just understood but embraced:

- *Clarity of Language:*

  They use straightforward and concise language to articulate the vision, avoiding ambiguity and ensuring everyone can comprehend the message.

- *Compelling Storytelling:*

  Extraordinary leaders weave compelling narratives around their vision, making it relatable and inspiring. Stories create an emotional connection that resonates deeply.

- *Visual Representation:*

  They utilize visual aids, such as charts, diagrams, or presentations, to provide a tangible representation of the vision, making it easier for others to grasp complex concepts.

- *Repetition with Purpose:*

  They consistently reinforce the key elements of the vision through repetition, ensuring that the core message becomes ingrained in the minds of their team.

- *Interactive Engagement:*

  Extraordinary leaders engage in open discussions and encourage questions, creating an interactive dialogue that clarifies any uncertainties and fosters a shared understanding.

- *Living by Example:*

  They embody the values and principles of the vision in their actions, serving as living examples of what it means to align with the overarching goals.

- *Feedback and Adjustments:*

  They actively seek feedback, recognizing that clarity can be a dynamic process. Adjustments are made based on insights and evolving circumstances to maintain a crystal-clear vision.

By employing these strategies, extraordinary leaders ensure that their vision is not just a concept but a vivid and actionable roadmap for everyone involved.

Beyond the visionary aspect, the profound impact of *clarity* and fulfillment extends to those under the guidance of extraordinary leaders. Here's how:

- *Inspired Confidence:*

  Clarity in the vision instills a sense of purpose and direction among team members, fostering confidence in their roles and the collective journey.

- *Motivation and Engagement:*

  When individuals find fulfillment in their contribution to a clear and meaningful vision, their motivation soars. They become actively engaged, driven by a shared sense of purpose.

- *Unified Collaboration:*

Clarity brings alignment, and fulfillment breeds enthusiasm. Together, these create a powerful synergy, promoting unified collaboration within the team toward common objectives.

- *Personal Growth Opportunities:*

Extraordinary leaders create an environment of clarity where individuals can clearly see their role in the bigger picture. This clarity opens doors for personal growth and development.

- *Resilience in Challenges:*

A clear and fulfilling vision serves as a source of resilience during challenging times. Team members, driven by a shared purpose, are more likely to weather storms and overcome obstacles.

- *Enhanced Well-Being:*

Individuals experiencing fulfillment in their work, fueled by a clear vision, often report higher levels of job satisfaction and overall well-being.

- *Legacy of Impact:*

    Clarity and fulfillment, when woven into the fabric of leadership, create a lasting impact. Team members become part of a legacy, contributing meaningfully to a shared vision that extends beyond immediate goals.

In reality, being clear and providing fulfillment affects more than just the leader. It improves the lives and experiences of everyone in the team. Clarity and fulfillment are important parts of guiding both the leader and the team's direction. Great leaders are known not just for setting goals but also for creating a work environment where everyone is happy and feels their work is valuable.

As we move to the next chapter, remember this: Being a leader isn't just about getting to the end goal. It's about making the journey meaningful, where every step matters and everyone in the team finds their own sense of purpose and satisfaction.

CHAPTER 2

Building Bigger Than You

In the world of leadership, there's a place where leaders think bigger than just their own goals. Welcome to Chapter 2, where we start a journey about more than just ourselves. It's about learning to "build bigger than you."

"Building bigger than you" leadership is characterized by a visionary mindset that sees beyond the confines of individual capabilities and aspirations, seeking to create a legacy that outlives the leader. Extraordinary leaders understand that true success is not just about personal achievements but about elevating others, fostering a culture of collaboration, and instilling a shared sense of purpose. Their approach is not limited to short-term goals; instead, they are architects of enduring change, building foundations that support and inspire future growth.

A great example of extraordinary leadership in business is Anne Mulcahy, who was CEO of Xerox. When she became CEO in 2001, Xerox was almost bankrupt. Instead of just fixing the company's finances, Mulcahy focused on changing its culture and values. She worked on empowering her team, listening to all employees, and getting everyone to share a common goal. This way, she made everyone feel part of the company's success, which had a big positive impact.

Mulcahy's time as CEO of Xerox shows how effective it is to think beyond just fixing immediate problems. She did more than just save the company; she gave her team a sense of belief and purpose. By the time she retired, Xerox wasn't just financially stable; it had also become a company focused on innovation and growth. This change continued even after she left, proving that extraordinary leadership is about having a lasting impact and influence, not just personal achievements. Mulcahy's leadership shows that building something bigger than yourself is about creating lasting change, not just short-term success.

Extraordinary leadership is the ability to expand influence and impact beyond personal boundaries is not just a skill—it's an art form. Here are some "Building bigger than you" strategies:

- *Strategic Networking:*

  Great leaders build a network of connections that go beyond their industry. Networking isn't just about getting contacts; it's about growing relationships that increase their impact.

- *Cross-Industry Collaboration:*

  By getting rid of barriers and encouraging teamwork across different industries, leaders make an impact that spreads far and reaches new areas.

- *Global Vision, Local Impact:*

  Extraordinary leaders think globally but act locally. By understanding and respecting the nuances of various communities, they tailor their impact to resonate on a personal level.

- *Mentorship and Legacy Building:*

  Investing in mentorship programs and nurturing emerging leaders isn't just about personal growth; it's about crafting a legacy that extends beyond individual achievements.

- *Media and Thought Leadership:*

  Leveraging media platforms and establishing thought leadership positions leaders as influencers in their field, allowing their ideas to permeate into broader audiences.

- *Digital Presence and Innovation:*

  A powerful digital presence is a conduit for influence. Extraordinary leaders leverage technology and innovation to amplify their voices, reaching audiences on a global scale.

- *Crisis Leadership and Social Impact:*

  Stepping into the arena of crisis leadership and championing social causes positions leaders as forces for positive change, expanding their impact into the fabric of societal transformation.

Making the vision bigger than yourself involves transcending personal ambitions and aligning it with a broader purpose. Here's how you can achieve that:

- *Clarify and Articulate a Grand Vision:*

  Define a vision that extends beyond immediate goals, encompassing a larger impact on your industry, community, or even society.

- *Connect Personal Values to the Vision:*

  Align the vision with your core values. When your personal values are embedded in the broader vision, it becomes a powerful force that goes beyond individual aspirations.

- *Think Long-Term and Sustainable:*

  Shift your perspective from short-term gains to long-term, sustainable impact. Consider how your actions today contribute to a lasting legacy.

- *Embrace Collaborative Leadership:*

  Foster a culture of collaboration where team members actively contribute to and feel ownership of the vision. This collective effort makes the vision inherently bigger than any individual.

- *Leverage Technology and Innovation:*

  Embrace technology and innovation to scale your impact. Whether through digital platforms or cutting-edge solutions, leverage these tools to reach a broader audience and make a more significant difference.

- *Cultivate a Global Mindset:*

  Expand your vision globally, even if your immediate impact is local. Consider how your work can resonate with and positively affect diverse communities around the world.

- *Prioritize Social and Environmental Impact:*

  Integrate social and environmental considerations into your vision. A vision that addresses broader societal or environmental challenges inherently transcends individual goals.

- *Seek Wisdom from Diverse Perspectives:*

  Surround yourself with diverse perspectives. Seeking input from people with varied backgrounds and experiences can enrich your vision and ensure it resonates on a broader scale.

Remember, making the vision bigger than yourself is a transformative journey. It requires a commitment to something greater than personal success, embracing the responsibility of leadership with a focus on positive, lasting impact.

Valuing your team's heart over their skill is a powerful approach to leadership that fosters a positive and collaborative work environment. Here are some strategies to prioritize the *heart* of your team:

- *Cultivate a Supportive Culture:*

  Foster a culture where team members feel valued for their unique qualities, contributions, and the care they bring to their work. Encourage open communication and mutual support.

- *Recognize and Appreciate Effort:*

  Acknowledge and appreciate the effort and dedication your team puts into their work. Celebrate milestones, both big and small, to show that you recognize the heart they invest in their tasks.

- *Emphasize Team Collaboration:*

  Place a strong emphasis on collaboration and teamwork. Highlight the importance of working together toward common goals, creating a sense of unity and shared purpose.

- *Encourage Work-Life Balance:*

  Demonstrate concern for your team members' well-being by encouraging a healthy work-life balance. Recognize the value of personal time and stress the importance of overall well-being.

- *Listen Actively:*

   Practice active listening. Understand your team members' perspectives, concerns, and aspirations. This not only shows that you value their input but also helps build a sense of trust and connection.

- *Provide Growth Opportunities:*

   Offer opportunities for personal and professional growth. Show that you are invested in the development of your team members beyond their technical skills, supporting their overall career aspirations.

- *Express Empathy and Compassion:*

   Demonstrate empathy and compassion in your leadership. Acknowledge and understand the personal challenges your team may face, and offer support in a genuine and caring manner.

- *Lead by Example:*

   Showcase the values of heart-centered leadership through your own actions. When your team sees that you prioritize relationships, empathy, and collaboration, they are more likely to follow suit.

- *Create a Positive Work Environment:*

  Foster a positive work environment where kindness, respect, and appreciation are integral. A positive atmosphere enhances team morale and encourages a heart-centered approach.

By consistently implementing these strategies, you create a workplace culture where the heart of each team member is valued, leading to increased motivation, job satisfaction, and overall team effectiveness.

As we conclude this chapter, here are some leadership affirmations that can serve as daily inspiration:

Leadership Affirmations:

> ➢ Catch the rhythm of collaboration, where every connection is a note in the melody of influence.

> ➢ Lead with a global perspective, but let your impact be felt in the heartbeat of local communities.

> ➢ In the dance of mentorship, every step leaves an imprint on the legacy of leadership.

> ➢ In the arena of thought leadership, your words echo, creating waves of influence.

> ➢ In the crucible of crisis, let your influence be the catalyst for societal transformation.

> ➢ Leadership isn't about the reach of an individual but the depth of impact created.

CHAPTER 3

The Benefits of Borrowed Influence

In this chapter, we delve into the dynamic interplay of influence—how borrowing it can be a powerful catalyst for transformative leadership.

In leadership, using others' influence is a game-changer. It takes us beyond what we can do alone. This approach is not about exploiting others, but rather about acknowledging and valuing the diverse skills and experiences that different individuals bring to the table. It involves a leader recognizing their own limitations and actively seeking the guidance, support, or partnership of others who possess the necessary skills or influence they lack. This can mean collaborating with more experienced colleagues, seeking mentorship, or aligning with influential figures within the industry.

"Borrowing influence" allows leaders to overcome personal and professional limitations, thereby facilitating more effective decision-making and problem-solving.

Take the example of Howard Schultz, the CEO of Starbucks, and his mentor, Warren Bennis, a renowned leadership expert. Schultz, while already successful, recognized the value of Bennis's extensive experience in leadership and organizational development. By aligning himself with Bennis, Schultz was able to gain invaluable insights into effective leadership and organizational management. This relationship helped Schultz in navigating the complexities of leading a global brand and in fostering a corporate culture that emphasized empathy and social responsibility. Bennis's influence is evident in Schultz's leadership style, which focuses on employee welfare and social impact, setting Starbucks apart in the corporate world.

This example demonstrates how borrowing influence can be a strategic move for leaders looking to expand their horizons and enhance their leadership skills. It underscores the idea that leadership is not just about personal attributes or individual achievements, but also about the ability to collaborate, learn from others, and incorporate diverse viewpoints into one's leadership approach.

Here are some of the benefits of "borrowed influence":

- *Collaborative Synergy:*

  When leaders share influence with each other, they work together better than they would alone. This teamwork becomes a strong force for making changes.

- *Cross-Pollination of Ideas:*

  Using others' influence lets leaders mix different ideas, experiences, and ways of doing things. This leads to new, creative solutions that go beyond what one person could think of alone.

- *Amplification of Impact:*

  Influence, when borrowed and shared, becomes a catalyst for amplifying impact. Leaders can collectively address larger challenges and make a more significant contribution to societal and organizational transformation.

- *Cultivation of Trust and Relationships:*

  Borrowing influence fosters trust and strengthens relationships among leaders. It's a reciprocal act that builds a network of trust, creating a foundation for future collaborative endeavors.

- *Adaptability and Resilience:*

  Leaders who borrow influence demonstrate adaptability and resilience. By drawing on a collective pool of strengths, they can navigate challenges more effectively, ensuring sustained success in dynamic environments.

- *Find Common Ground:*

Before starting, find common values with those you're working with. Building on shared beliefs makes it easier to combine ideas.

- *Clear Communication:*

Communicate openly and clearly. Share your goals, expectations, and the benefits of working together to build trust and understanding.

- *Listen Well:*

Pay attention to others' ideas and views. Understanding them is key to creating a successful group effort.

- *Choose Partners Wisely:*

Pick partners who have strengths that work well with yours for a better overall result.

- *Welcome Different Ideas:*

Be open to a variety of thoughts and approaches. This adds richness and complexity to your work together.

- *Share Influence:*

Make sharing influence a two-way street. Recognize that everyone has unique strengths to offer.

- *Celebrate Together:*

  Celebrate your joint achievements. Show appreciation for the group's impact in reaching goals.

- *Keep Learning:*

  See this as a chance to keep learning and improving. Change and grow with feedback from your group.

- *Be Patient:*

  Understand that good things take time. Enjoy the process of working together and creating something meaningful.

Leadership Affirmations:

- *Borrowed influence is the sheet music that guides us in this collaborative composition.*

- *In the garden of borrowed influence, ideas bloom into a vibrant landscape of creativity and progress.*

- *As leaders borrow and lend influence, they invest in a currency that multiplies impact exponentially.*

- *Borrowed influence isn't just a loan; it's an investment that multiplies impact exponentially.*

- *Trust, minted with every exchange of borrowed influence, becomes the foundation for future collaborative endeavors.*

- *In the symphony of borrowed influence, collaborative notes create a resonance that echoes far beyond individual melodies.*

- *In the garden of borrowed influence, ideas bloom into a vibrant landscape of creativity and progress.*

- *Borrowed influence isn't just a loan; it's an investment that multiplies impact exponentially.*

> ➤ *In the currency of borrowed influence, trust is minted with every exchange.*

> ➤ *In the dance of borrowed influence, adaptability becomes the rhythm that ensures resilience.*

CHAPTER 4

Building Teams that Resonate

As we transition to the next step in our exploration of extraordinary leadership, let's venture into the art of "building teams that resonate."

Picture a team working together perfectly, with everyone using their special skills to create great teamwork. It's a great vision, but it's not the easiest thing to do. Turning a group of people into a strong, effective team is a process that goes beyond just assembling talents; it involves cultivating an environment of collaboration, trust, and shared purpose.

The first step in this transformation is establishing clear and attainable goals, ensuring every team member understands not only what is expected of them but also how their contributions fit into the larger picture. Communication is key: open, honest, and frequent interactions foster a sense of transparency and unity. Leaders should encourage team members to voice their ideas and concerns, creating a culture where diverse perspectives are not only heard but valued. It's also crucial to recognize and leverage the unique strengths of each individual, aligning their skills and passions with the team's objectives. This alignment not only maximizes efficiency but also enhances job satisfaction and engagement.

Beyond achieving goals, building a team that makes a lasting impression involves nurturing a sense of camaraderie and collective achievement. Celebrating milestones, no matter how small, can boost morale and reinforce a sense of team identity. Handling conflicts constructively is equally important; a team that learns to resolve disagreements respectfully and effectively becomes more resilient and adaptable. Encouraging continuous learning and development helps the team stay innovative and prepared for future challenges. By investing in team-building activities and creating opportunities for personal and professional growth, leaders can foster a supportive and dynamic environment.

Ultimately, a team that not only meets its goals but leaves a lasting impression is one that operates with a blend of mutual respect, shared commitment, and an unwavering focus on both individual and collective growth.

Let's explore how to turn a group of people into a strong, effective team—a team that not only meets its goals but also makes a lasting impression along the way.

- *Vision as the Melody:*

  The leader serves as the conductor, wielding the vision as the melody that unites every instrument in the team. A clear and compelling vision becomes the guiding force that harmonizes individual efforts.

- *Diverse Instruments, Unified Purpose:*

Embrace the diversity of talents within the team, recognizing that each member is a unique instrument. The challenge lies in orchestrating this diversity toward a unified purpose, creating a symphony of collaboration.

- *Cultivating Trust:*

Trust is the adhesive that binds the team together. Building trust requires open communication, reliability, and a shared commitment to the collective success of the team.

- *Encouraging Individual Flourish:*

Like how every instrument gets a solo, let each team member show their strengths. A good team lets everyone's skills add to the group's success.

- *Active Listening and Responsive Harmony:*

Foster a culture of active listening, where team members respond to one another with flexibility and adaptability. This responsive harmony allows the team to adjust and flourish in dynamic environments.

- *Celebrating Milestones:*

   Celebrate big and small wins in your teamwork. Praise both individual and group successes to create an encouraging and motivating environment.

- *Constantly Working to Get Better:*

   Just as an orchestra practices regularly, a good team constantly tries to improve. Regular reviews, feedback, and a focus on learning help the team perform at its best.

Your role as a leader is to guide your team to make a significant and lasting impact. Building teams that resonate is about finding the right balance of trust, communication, shared values, and a common goal. Think of your team as a group where each member plays a crucial role in achieving success. Trust is the foundation, creating a sense of reliance and confidence among team members. As a leader, you're responsible for building and maintaining this trust.

Communication is key in every interaction. It's your job to ensure clear and open communication, making sure everyone's voice is heard and valued. Shared values are like guidelines that steer the team's behavior and decisions, creating a unified culture. As a leader, you must communicate and uphold these values.

The team's shared goal is what brings everyone together. It's up to you to present a clear and compelling vision and objectives. Team members should understand how their work contributes to the larger mission, giving their efforts more meaning and motivation.

Collaboration is vital. It's important to create an inclusive environment where different perspectives and strengths are combined to achieve the best results. Recognizing and appreciating each member's contributions is also crucial. Regularly acknowledging achievements fosters a positive atmosphere and a culture of appreciation.

A commitment to continuous learning and growth is essential. Teams should learn from both successes and failures, with leaders encouraging a mindset of curiosity and improvement. Emotional intelligence is also important, as it helps in understanding and responding to the team's emotional needs, building a supportive environment.

Flexibility and adaptability are necessary for navigating changes smoothly. As a leader, you should guide your team through these transitions with ease. Regular feedback, both giving and receiving, is important for ongoing improvement and refining team performance.

Regular feedback is the ongoing dialogue. Leaders provide constructive insights, and team members contribute their thoughts. This feedback loop creates an environment of continuous improvement. Maintaining a healthy team is an ongoing process that requires proactive leadership and a commitment to fostering a positive work environment.

Here's a narrative approach on how to keep your team healthy:

As the leader, envision your role as that of a caretaker tending to a vibrant garden. Just as a gardener nurtures the soil, waters the plants, and ensures they receive ample sunlight, your role involves cultivating the conditions for a thriving team.

Start by tending to the soil of trust. Just as a healthy garden needs fertile soil, your team flourishes in an environment built on trust. Cultivate openness and transparency, allowing trust to take root and create a solid foundation for collaboration.

Water your team with clear communication. Imagine communication as the lifeblood that sustains your garden. Regularly provide nourishment by sharing information, setting clear expectations, and fostering open dialogue. This ensures that each team member is well-informed and aligned with the collective vision.

Sow the seeds of shared values. Your team, much like a diverse array of plants, flourishes when rooted in common values. Clearly articulate these values and weave them into the fabric of your team's culture. This shared ethical soil becomes the bedrock for a healthy and cohesive unit.

Nurture a sense of collective purpose. Envision your team's mission as the guiding North Star. Just as plants lean toward the sunlight, team members gravitate toward a shared purpose. Reinforce this purpose regularly, aligning individual efforts with the overarching goal, creating a sense of direction and motivation.

Promote collaborative growth. Picture your team as an ecosystem where different species thrive together. Encourage collaboration by recognizing and leveraging each member's unique strengths. Like diverse plant species complementing each other, diverse talents contribute to a vibrant and resilient team.

Celebrate achievements as blooming flowers. Just as a garden bursts into color during the blooming season, acknowledge and celebrate your team's successes. Whether big or small, these achievements are the vibrant flowers that add color and joy to your team's journey.

Ensure continuous learning as a nurturing breeze. Imagine a gentle breeze that stimulates growth and learning. Foster a culture where your team feels encouraged to explore new ideas, learn from experiences, and adapt to change. This constant breeze of learning keeps your team agile and resilient.

Cultivate emotional well-being. Consider the emotional well-being of your team as the sunlight that sustains growth. Be attuned to the emotional needs of your team members, offering support and creating an environment where their mental health is prioritized.

Adaptability as the flexibility of branches. Just as branches sway in the wind, encourage adaptability within your team. Embrace change, adjust strategies when needed, and foster flexibility. This adaptability ensures that your team remains resilient in the face of challenges.

Establish a feedback loop as the rhythm of growth. Envision feedback as the rhythmic pulse that guides your team's growth. Regularly provide constructive feedback and create opportunities for team members to share their thoughts. This continuous dialogue enhances your team's performance and strengthens its cohesiveness.

In nurturing your team as a garden, remember that it's an ongoing process. Regular care, attention, and a deep understanding of your team's unique dynamics contribute to its sustained health and vitality. As the gardener of your team, your commitment to fostering a positive and thriving environment ensures a bountiful harvest of success and collaboration.

Leadership Affirmations:

➢ *As leaders, we are not merely architects of tasks but conductors orchestrating a collective masterpiece.*

➢ *In the orchestra of teamwork, diverse instruments blend to create a rich and harmonious composition.*

➢ *Trust, like a resonant chord, forms the foundation of a harmonious team.*

➢ *In the symphony of teamwork, milestones become powerful crescendos that resonate with shared achievement.*

➢ *In the symphony of teamwork, continuous rehearsal sharpens the team's ability to resonate with excellence.*

CHAPTER 5

Unlocking the Power of Borrowed Brilliance

In leadership, true brilliance comes from combining everyone's smart ideas, not just from one person's talent. This chapter is about leaders gathering insights from various sources to build a landscape of innovation and outstanding performance by "borrowing brilliance."

In his best-selling book *Borrowing Brilliance: The Six Steps to Business Innovation by Building on the Ideas of Others,* author David Kord Murray explains, "Ideas are born of other ideas, built in and out of the ideas that came before." That is the essence of "borrowed brilliance."

"Some of the most creative people who have ever lived, such as Isaac Newton and William Shakespeare, were accused of idea theft and plagiarism," says Murray. "Ideas, like species, naturally evolve over time. Existing concepts are altered and combined to construct new concepts; the way geometry, trigonometry, and algebra combine to form calculus."

With that in mind, here are some of the benefits of applying "borrowed brilliance" to leadership roles:

- *Collaborative Sparks of Innovation:*

  Borrowed brilliance ignites collaborative sparks, where ideas fuse and evolve into innovative breakthroughs. Leaders who draw from a diverse pool of brilliance create a symphony of ingenuity that transcends individual limitations.

- *Cross-Pollination of Expertise:*

  Borrowing brilliance involves cross-pollinating expertise across disciplines. Leaders who explore and integrate insights from diverse fields enrich their own understanding, fostering a culture where brilliance blossoms through interdisciplinary collaboration.

- *Shared Wisdom, Shared Success:*

  Wisdom borrowed is wisdom multiplied. Leaders who seek and share wisdom from mentors, peers, and other sources create a reservoir of shared insights, paving the way for shared success.

- *Adaptive Learning Networks:*

  Building adaptive learning networks allows leaders to tap into the brilliance of others. These networks become dynamic ecosystems where knowledge flows freely, propelling continuous growth and adaptability.

- *Inspirational Role Models:*

Leaders who borrow brilliance often find inspiration in role models. By studying the success stories of others, leaders glean insights and motivation, shaping their own journey toward greatness.

- *Collective Problem-Solving:*

Borrowed brilliance transforms problem-solving into a collective endeavor. Leaders who invite diverse perspectives and solutions create a collaborative symphony where challenges are met with ingenious, collective solutions.

- *Innovation Catalyst:*

Borrowed brilliance acts as a spark for innovation. Drawing inspiration and insights from diverse sources fuels creative thinking, propelling you to approach challenges with fresh perspectives and inventive solutions.

- *Continuous Learning Engine:*

Embracing borrowed brilliance fosters a culture of continuous learning. By seeking wisdom from mentors, learning from others' experiences, and tapping into diverse knowledge networks, you cultivate a mindset of perpetual growth.

- *Adaptive Leadership Agility:*

  Borrowed brilliance enhances adaptive leadership agility. Leveraging the collective intelligence of others allows you to navigate uncertainties and change with resilience, as you draw upon a diverse range of skills, perspectives, and solutions.

- *Global Vision and Cultural Fluency:*

  Engaging with borrowed brilliance on a global scale shapes your leadership with a broadened worldview. Cultural fluency and global vision become integral, enabling you to lead in an interconnected world with sensitivity and understanding.

- *Collaborative Synergy:*

  Harnessing borrowed brilliance creates collaborative synergy within your team. Encouraging a culture where diverse ideas are valued and shared fosters a harmonious environment where each team member contributes to the collective brilliance.

- *Strategic Decision-Making:*

  Borrowed brilliance informs strategic decision-making. Drawing on insights from mentors, industry experts, and diverse perspectives empowers you to make informed and strategic choices that align with the complexities of your leadership journey.

- *Resilience Through Adversity:*

  Borrowed brilliance acts as a source of resilience in the face of adversity. Learning from others' challenges and setbacks provides valuable lessons, enabling you to navigate difficulties with a fortified mindset and adaptive strategies.

- *Elevated Mentorship and Role Modeling:*

  Embracing borrowed brilliance allows you to elevate your mentorship and role modeling. By incorporating the wisdom of those who have gone before, you enhance your capacity to guide and inspire others, creating a positive impact on the development of emerging leaders.

- *Shared Vision Crafting:*

  The influence of borrowed brilliance shapes your ability to craft a shared vision. Involving others in the vision-setting process taps into a collective genius, aligning the team toward a common purpose that resonates with shared brilliance.

- *Cultivation of Learning Communities:*

  Establishing learning communities becomes a cornerstone of your leadership. Through borrowed brilliance, you foster environments where shared insights, reflections, and collaborative growth are valued, creating a learning culture that transcends individual brilliance.

By integrating "borrowed brilliance" and the ideas of others who have come before into your leadership mantra, you amplify your impact and shape a legacy that transcends individual accomplishment. How do you envision integrating borrowed brilliance into your leadership journey?

Borrowed brilliance transforms leadership by catalyzing innovation, fostering continuous learning, and instilling adaptive agility. It broadens your global vision, shapes collaborative synergy, and fortifies your resilience in the face of challenges. Embracing borrowed brilliance enables strategic decision-making, elevates mentorship, and guides the crafting of a shared vision.

Leadership Affirmations:

➤ *In the mosaic of leadership, collaborative sparks illuminate the path to innovative brilliance.*

➤ *In the garden of leadership, cross-pollination nurtures a vibrant bloom of collective expertise.*

➤ *In the library of leadership, borrowed wisdom becomes the cornerstone of shared success.*

➤ *In the network of leadership, adaptive learning becomes the currency of borrowed brilliance.*

➤ *In the portrait of leadership, borrowed brilliance paints an inspiring canvas of role models.*

➤ *In the puzzle of leadership, borrowed brilliance pieces together solutions that transcend individual puzzles.*

CHAPTER 6

Orchestrating Influence and Impact

Influence plays a pivotal role in shaping a leader and the culture they foster within their organization, and real-life business examples further illuminate this.

Take Satya Nadella, CEO of Microsoft, for instance. His influence has been instrumental in transforming Microsoft's culture. When he took over, he shifted the focus from individual achievements to collaboration and growth. His approach to leadership, emphasizing empathy and teamwork, has not only won him trust and respect but has also fostered a more innovative and inclusive culture at Microsoft.

Another example is Indra Nooyi, the former CEO of PepsiCo. Her influence extended beyond traditional business metrics; she championed a health-focused shift in the company's product line, demonstrating a commitment to consumer health and environmental sustainability. This move, rooted in her personal convictions, influenced PepsiCo's culture, encouraging a broader perspective on business success that includes social responsibility.

In the tech industry, the influence of Apple's late CEO, Steve Jobs, is a testament to how a leader's vision can shape a company's culture. Jobs' emphasis on design excellence and innovation became core values at Apple, propelling the company to unprecedented heights. His influence created a culture where pushing boundaries and striving for perfection became the norm, which continues to drive Apple's success.

Sheryl Sandberg, COO of Facebook, is another leader whose influence has been critical, especially in advocating for women in the workplace. Her book, *Lean In*, and her work at Facebook have inspired a culture of gender equality and empowerment, not just within Facebook but in the wider corporate world. Her influence has encouraged leaders to rethink their organizational culture and policies regarding diversity and inclusion.

In the world of e-commerce, Jeff Bezos of Amazon has used his influence to create a culture of innovation and customer obsession. His leadership style, which encourages thinking big and being customer-centric, has been a key factor in Amazon's growth. The culture at Amazon, driven by Bezos' influence, is one where new ideas are encouraged and customer satisfaction is paramount.

These leaders demonstrate that influence is a powerful tool in shaping organizational culture. It's about leading by example, setting values and standards that permeate the entire organization, and inspiring change that aligns with these values. The impact of their influence is seen in the way their organizations operate, the products they create, and the industry standards they set, showcasing the profound effect a leader can have on their organization's culture and success.

All of these highly successful leaders have their own "secret sauce" to success. Here are some practical ways you can continue to build your own leadership style:

- *Strategic Stakeholder Engagement:*

  Working well with stakeholders means leaders need to build strong relationships that help everyone work together better. It's about getting everyone to agree on common goals and to cooperate effectively.

- *Visionary Leadership Narrative:*

  Having a clear and inspiring vision is important for leaders. It helps motivate everyone to work towards the same goals. A good leader makes sure their vision is understood and shared by the whole team.

- *Cultivating a Culture of Empowerment:*

  Leaders should create an environment where every team member feels confident and valued. This means letting everyone use their skills to the fullest, which helps the whole team do better.

- *Authenticity in Leadership:*

  Being genuine and honest is important for leaders. When leaders are true to themselves and their team, it builds trust and makes them more effective.

- *Strategic Communication:*

  Good communication is essential for leaders. It means making sure messages are clear and understood by everyone. This helps keep the team focused and moving towards the same objectives.

- *Adapting to Change:*

  Leaders need to be able to handle change well. They should guide their team through new situations smoothly and keep them focused on their goals, even when things are shifting.

Let's break down influence and impact in simpler terms:

Influence is about changing how people see things, make decisions, and act, using inspiration, persuasion, and good people skills. It means guiding and motivating others to work together towards a common goal or vision.

- *Nature of Influence:*

  Influence comes from being good at communicating, understanding others' feelings, and connecting with people on a deeper level. It's a gentle yet powerful way to guide people's thoughts and actions.

- *Scope of Influence:*

  Influence works on thoughts and attitudes. It changes how people think and decide, guiding group understanding and behavior without being obvious.

Impact:

Impact is the clear, significant result of what you do, decide, or influence. It's the visible change or effect that happens because of a leader's actions, affecting individuals, teams, or whole organizations.

- *Nature of Impact:*

  Impact is the clear evidence of good leadership. It shows up as real changes in how people behave, how well they perform, or in the results of an organization. It's about making a real difference.

- *Scope of Impact:*

  Impact has long-lasting effects. It's the lasting mark of a leader's work, showing the success and power of their leadership over time.

Relationship:

- *Influence leads to Impact:*

  Influence prepares the way for impact. Using influence well creates the right conditions for significant and positive changes to happen.

- *Impact finishes what Influence starts:*

  Impact is what you see after using influence. It's the visible, lasting change that comes from effectively guiding and inspiring others.

Understanding how influence and impact work together helps leaders manage the complex parts of leading. It shows that being able to communicate well, understand others, and connect with them is crucial for shaping how people think and, ultimately, for making a lasting positive difference. How do you think these ideas fit into your own leadership style?

CHAPTER 7

The Connection of Leadership

Connection is crucial for top-notch leadership. It means building real, strong relationships with your team and others. Great leaders don't just know people—they understand them. This helps them motivate their team better, making everyone more productive and happy at work. A leader who connects well, is easy to talk to, and cares about their team. This makes everyone more open and willing to share ideas.

In today's fast-paced world, being able to connect well helps leaders keep their team strong and flexible. When things get tough, like in a crisis, a well-connected leader can guide their team more effectively. These strong bonds also make it easier for the team to work together and come up with new ideas. Leaders who focus on connection can also sense problems early and fix them quickly.

Connection is also key for leaders to make a bigger impact. Good leaders use their relationships to learn new things and find chances to grow. They can get advice, work together with others, and get support for their plans. In short, connection helps leaders build a supportive network, create a positive work environment, and lead with a vision that inspires everyone. This is what makes a leader truly great.

Here are a few ways that can help leaders can create connection:

- *Authenticity:*

  Be genuine and authentic. People resonate with sincerity, and authenticity forms the foundation for meaningful connections.

- *Active Listening:*

  Practice active listening. Truly understanding others fosters a sense of being heard and valued, strengthening the connection.

- *Empathy:*

  Cultivate empathy. Put yourself in others' shoes to understand their perspectives and feelings, creating a deeper and more compassionate connection.

- *Open Communication:*

  Foster open communication. Encourage dialogue where ideas and feelings can be freely expressed, building an atmosphere of trust and connection.

- *Shared Values:*

  Identify shared values. Common ground provides a solid foundation for connection, allowing individuals to align around shared principles.

- *Recognition and Appreciation:*

  Acknowledge and appreciate others. Recognizing their contributions and expressing gratitude strengthens the bond and creates a positive connection.

- *Vulnerability:*

  Be willing to show vulnerability. Opening up about your own experiences and challenges creates an atmosphere of trust and reciprocity.

- *Consistency:*

  Be consistent in your interactions. Regular and reliable communication helps build a sense of dependability and strengthens connections over time.

- *Quality Time:*

  Invest quality time in relationships. Whether in one-on-one conversations or team activities, dedicating time fosters stronger and more meaningful connections.

- *Celebrate Successes:*

  Celebrate achievements together. Sharing in successes reinforces the sense of camaraderie and strengthens the bond within the group.

- *Respect Differences:*

  Embrace diversity and respect differences. Recognizing and appreciating diverse perspectives enriches connections and contributes to a more inclusive environment.

- *Offer Support:*

  Be supportive in times of need. Offering assistance and demonstrating care during challenging moments deepens connections and builds a sense of community.

  Remember, building connections is an ongoing process that requires attention, care, and a genuine interest in others.

- *Trust and Collaboration:*

  Relationships are the bedrock of trust. Trust is essential for effective collaboration and teamwork. Strong relationships foster an environment where team members feel confident in each other's abilities, leading to enhanced collaboration and collective success.

- *Employee Engagement:*

  Positive relationships contribute to higher employee engagement. When leaders build genuine connections with their team members, it creates a sense of belonging and purpose, which, in turn, boosts motivation and commitment.

- *Effective Communication:*

  Relationships facilitate open and effective communication. A culture of strong relationships encourages transparent and honest communication, reducing misunderstandings and fostering a healthy exchange of ideas.

- *Resilience in Challenges:*

  During challenging times, relationships serve as a support system. Teams with strong interpersonal connections are more resilient, helping each other navigate obstacles and maintain morale in the face of adversity.

- *Innovation and Creativity:*

  Collaborative relationships spur innovation. When team members feel comfortable expressing their ideas and opinions, it leads to a more creative and innovative environment where diverse perspectives contribute to problem-solving and ideation.

- *Employee Well-Being:*

  Strong relationships contribute to employee well-being. Feeling valued and supported at work positively impacts mental health and overall job satisfaction, creating a positive workplace culture.

- *Retention and Loyalty:*

  Employees are more likely to stay with a company where they have strong relationships. A positive workplace culture, characterized by meaningful connections, fosters loyalty and reduces turnover.

- *Adaptability and Change Management:*

  Relationships enhance adaptability to change. When there's a foundation of trust and mutual understanding, teams are more likely to embrace change and navigate transitions effectively.

- *Conflict Resolution:*

  Healthy relationships provide a framework for resolving conflicts. Teams with strong interpersonal connections are better equipped to address disagreements constructively, finding solutions that benefit the entire group.

- *Leadership Effectiveness:*

  Leaders who prioritize relationships are often more effective. Building trust, understanding team dynamics, and connecting with individuals on a personal level contribute to leadership success.

Basically, relationships are what hold a strong and lasting team together. Whether dealing with tough times or enjoying good times, how well the team members get along plays a big part in how well the team works. As a leader, it's really important to focus on making and keeping good relationships. This helps in creating a positive and successful team. How have relationships affected your experience as a leader?

CHAPTER 8

The Importance of Sustaining Great Leadership

You've taken the time to learn how to become a better leader, and you've implemented some of the traits we have talked about throughout this book. Now comes the hard part—sustaining it for the long haul. Keeping a strong leadership culture in an organization is key. This culture is like the foundation of a successful company. It shows everyone how things should be done and how people should work together. It's not just about having leaders; it's about making a place where everyone is encouraged to be a leader in their own way. This helps everyone understand and work towards the company's goals and values.

In today's fast-changing business world, a strong leadership culture is critical to adapt and stay strong. Companies with good leadership can better handle challenges and changes, like new market trends or customer needs. This culture also encourages new ideas and taking risks, which is important for staying ahead in the industry.

Lastly, a strong leadership culture makes the company look good to others, like customers and business partners. A company known for good leadership is seen as trustworthy and modern. This good image helps the company do better in business and be more successful overall. In short, a strong leadership culture affects every part of the business, from how things run inside to how the company is seen from the outside.

An impressive example of a leader who has sustained excellence over time is Alan Mulally, the former CEO of Ford Motor Company. Mulally served as the CEO from 2006 to 2014, a period marked by significant challenges in the automotive industry, especially the 2008 financial crisis. His leadership during these turbulent times is a noteworthy example of maintaining excellence through strategic foresight, effective communication, and a strong focus on teamwork.

When Mulally took over at Ford, the company was facing severe financial difficulties. He immediately implemented a comprehensive turnaround plan, focusing on simplifying the brand's portfolio, improving the quality of its vehicles, and restoring its financial health. His "One Ford" plan was instrumental in this regard. This strategy emphasized a global approach to the business, streamlined operations, and fostered a more unified company culture. Mulally's focus on transparency and open communication played a crucial role in changing Ford's corporate culture. He established a system where managers were encouraged to honestly report problems, breaking down the silos and fear of sharing bad news that had previously hindered the company's progress.

Under Mulally's leadership, Ford was the only major American car manufacturer that didn't take a government bailout during the 2008 financial crisis. He guided the company through this period with strategic decisions like mortgaging assets early on to raise capital, which proved to be a critical move in keeping the company afloat. By the time he retired in 2014, Ford had achieved 19 consecutive quarters of profitability, a remarkable turnaround from the losses it was incurring when he took over. Mulally's leadership journey at Ford is a valuable lesson in how resilience, adaptability, and a strong team-oriented approach can lead a company to thrive even in the most challenging circumstances.

Here are some of the traits of some of the things that have allowed some of the best leaders to sustain their winning culture:

- *Legacy Building:*

  Explore how your leadership leaves an enduring imprint. What legacy are you crafting, and how can each decision echo in the annals of your team's history?

- *Continuous Learning:*

  Leadership is a lifelong learning experience. How can you embrace a mindset of continuous improvement and learning, ensuring that each new note is a chance to grow?

- *Adaptability and Resilience:*

  Adaptability and resilience are crucial for sustaining strong leadership, as they enable leaders to navigate challenges and changes effectively, maintaining their effectiveness and guiding their teams through uncertain times.

- *Mentorship and Developing Future Leaders:*

  Focus on helping new leaders grow. Teaching them and sharing your experience will ensure the team continues to thrive and succeed.

- *Recognizing Successes:*

  Celebrate your team's achievements. Remembering both the successes and challenges helps you understand what makes your leadership effective.

- *Embracing Different Talents:*

  Value the diverse abilities and views within your team. Making sure everyone's strengths are used well is important for a strong and united team.

- *Being Grateful and Reflective:*

  Take time to be grateful and think about your leadership journey. Acknowledge the people who have helped along the way and show your appreciation for their support in your success.

An effective leader understands the importance of "passing the baton" to sustain a legacy of strong business culture, recognizing that the continuity of leadership is as crucial as its current state. This process involves identifying and nurturing potential leaders within the organization, ensuring a seamless transition of roles and responsibilities. An insightful leader actively seeks out individuals who not only have the necessary skills and aptitude but also embody the core values and vision of the company. By investing in their development through mentorship, training, and providing challenging opportunities, the leader prepares them to carry forward the organizational ethos. This proactive approach not only secures the future of the company but also instills a sense of responsibility and belonging among upcoming leaders, making the transition more organic and effective.

Passing the baton also entails creating an environment where leadership is seen as a shared responsibility, rather than a solitary role at the top. An effective leader fosters a culture of collaboration, where team members are encouraged to take initiative and contribute their ideas. This democratic approach to leadership cultivates a sense of ownership among employees, as they feel their input is valued and can make a real difference. By involving team members in decision-making processes and strategic discussions, the leader demonstrates trust in their capabilities. This not only boosts morale and motivation but also provides hands-on experience in leadership roles, preparing them for future responsibilities. Additionally, this inclusive culture ensures that the company's values and practices are deeply ingrained in its people, making the eventual transition of leadership smoother and more aligned with the company's long-term goals.

An effective leader ensures that the process of passing the baton is continuous and not confined to the end of their tenure. This ongoing process is marked by constant communication, feedback, and reassessment of leadership needs and potentials within the team. Leaders must be keen observers, identifying and addressing gaps in skills or knowledge that might hinder the future leaders' ability to succeed. This forward-thinking approach not only builds a resilient pipeline of leadership talent but also demonstrates a commitment to the long-term success of the organization. The leader's ability to recognize and cultivate potential, create an empowering environment, and ensure a consistent focus on leadership development is what truly sustains a legacy of strong business culture, making the organization robust and adaptable for future challenges.

Leadership Affirmations:

➢ As a leader, legacy building involves more than achieving immediate success. It's about orchestrating decisions that stand the test of time.

➢ Legacy is the art of crafting decisions that don't just succeed today but compose a melody that echoes in the rhythm of leadership tomorrow.

➢ Passing the baton gracefully is an acknowledgment that leadership is a relay, not a sprint.

➢ A compelling legacy is an inspiration, a narrative that motivates individuals to contribute their best.

➢ Legacy is the motivational prelude that encourages every team member to play their part with passion, knowing they contribute to a greater masterpiece.

CONCLUSION

Gratitude

We've discussed many areas and aspects of improving your leadership skills and building a winning culture in this book. But I want to end with something a little less tangible—gratitude.

Gratitude is a key part of being a good leader. It's more than just being polite; it shows you recognize and value everyone's hard work and what they bring to the team. When leaders say thank you, it not only makes team members feel good and motivated, but it also brings everyone closer together, creating a stronger and more supportive environment.

Gratitude also shows that a leader understands success is a team effort. It's important to remember and appreciate everyone who helped along the way. This helps build a respectful and supportive culture in the team. Being grateful helps the leader stay positive and resilient, especially during tough times. It means focusing on the good things and the potential for growth, which can really boost the team's morale and outlook.

A business leader who has notably incorporated gratitude into their leadership style is Ken Chenault, the former CEO and Chairman of American Express. Chenault, who led the company from 2001 to 2018, is widely recognized not just for his exceptional leadership skills but also for his deep sense of gratitude towards his employees and community.

Throughout his tenure, Chenault frequently acknowledged and expressed appreciation for the hard work and dedication of his employees. He was known for his approachable and personable leadership style, often taking the time to connect with employees at all levels of the organization. This open and appreciative communication style helped to build a strong and inclusive company culture at American Express.

Chenault also demonstrated gratitude through his commitment to employee development and well-being. He was a strong advocate for diversity and inclusion, understanding that a diverse workforce was not just a moral imperative but also a business strength. Under his leadership, American Express was frequently listed as a top company for diversity and employee satisfaction.

Moreover, Chenault's sense of gratitude extended to the broader community. He was actively involved in various philanthropic activities and encouraged corporate social responsibility at American Express. For instance, under his leadership, the company supported community service programs and initiatives that contributed to social and cultural causes.

Ken Chenault's legacy is a testament to the fact that gratitude and appreciation are powerful tools in building a positive, productive, and socially responsible workplace.

Adding gratitude to *your* daily leadership is easy. It can be a simple thank you note, a shout-out in a meeting, or just listening to your team members. The key is to make saying thanks a regular thing, not just something special. This creates an environment where everyone feels safe and valued, and they'll do their best work.

Gratitude is not a one-time gesture; it's an ongoing practice. Leaders who consistently express gratitude contribute to the cultivation of a positive organizational culture. This culture becomes a breeding ground for creativity, innovation, and high levels of employee engagement, as team members feel a deep sense of connection and loyalty.

Expressing gratitude builds authentic relationships. It goes beyond formalities, creating a genuine connection between leaders and team members. This authenticity contributes to a positive leadership presence, fostering trust and openness within the team.

So, as we wrap up, think about how saying thank you can make a big difference in your role as a leader. It's a small thing, but it has a big impact on your style and on your team's culture. Keep this in mind as you continue to grow and lead, and remember the power of a simple thank you.

Thank you for reading this book, and I hope your journey in leadership is full of learning, growth, and plenty of chances to be grateful and appreciated.

Made in the USA
Columbia, SC
11 February 2025

53296582R10052